Pathways to Publishing
Self Publishing
Manuscript to Publication

by Branch Isole

Pathways to Publishing
Self Publishing
Manuscript to Publication
by Branch Isole

ISBN 978-0982658567
Library of Congress
Control Number: 2010912042

MANA'O PUBLISHING

Home of the VOYEURISTIC POET

Manao Publishing
Hampton, VA 23666

Order copies of this book at
www.branchisole.com
www.manaopublishing.com

For CC

If not for you
this would all be different.

Table of Contents

Introduction

As an aspiring writer I knew I wanted to test my works in the public domain where critique and consumption take place. After paying too much for a 'vanity' publisher's services, I learned the steps of self publishing.

No part of this book in isolation or as a whole will guarantee publication of your thoughts, ideas, opinions or works. However this Step-by-Step Guide will help you navigate the path to successful self publishing. I did it. You can too.

As of this writing, digital eBooks generate between six and eight percent of publishing revenues. This will change exponentially over the next fifty years.

By the time my grandchildren are my age I believe printed books will be collectors' items seen only at auctions, museums and in personal libraries.

Branch Isole

"Publication is the auction
of the Mind of Man."

~Emily Dickinson

Ask yourself-
What is my writing?
Is my writing a hobby or more?
Is my writing a craft or profession?
Answering these questions may save you time, effort, expense and energy.

Writing is not easy. Good writing is harder still and exceptional writing, like all fields of artistic endeavour succeeds only if and when an audience is found and the spark of recognition by readers is fanned to flaming.

Now ask yourself again-
Is my writing a hobby? . . . Or more?
Do I want to make money with my writing?
Do I intend to make a living from my writing?

If you answered "Yes" to these and you believe it understand this; writing at sustainable income levels takes the hours and dedication of a full time job, if not more. In addition you will be the one responsible to insure every item which needs to be accomplished is handled. You will need to initiate and complete all tasks yourself or with assistance, be it paid or not.

If your answer is now "No" congratulations!
If being honest with your answers makes you realize a dream of exceptional income levels and authorship success may be just a dream, great.
Without our dreams we accomplish nothing extraordinary.

Still interested in self publishing?
Here's the good news!
Even if your writing is a hobby and you are not looking for best seller status, the step-by-step process described in this book will help you get your book printed and into the hands of your fans and readers. If you want exposure of your writing to be fruitful and fulfilling for you and others, read on.

Chapter 1
Ways and Means

"Persistence breaks down resistance,
always has, always will."

Technology has made publishing a book easier than ever before. It is however, just as much work as in the past and the likelihood of being read by a large (paying) audience is as difficult as always to acquire.

Today there are five primary vehicles you can use to publish your book. Five distinctly different processes and yet the goal of all five is exactly the same; to sell as many books as possible. The legwork involved with all five choices is similar as well; through your efforts as author and marketer. Finally, the commercial success involved with all five is produced by the same end result; how many people are willingly to spend money to read your words.

Five ways to publish your book today;
1. Contract with a major publisher.
2. Contract with a smaller, independent or university press.
3. Contract with a 'Vanity' publisher.
4. Self publish.
5. Copy and bind.

Groups 1, 2, and 3 are not your friends. They are in business to make money from you, from your efforts and from your readers. This is not a personal attack on my part. It is a statement of fact. These corporations and businesses provide products and services 'for hire.' They are in business to make profits, not friends.

For a moment let's examine the general Pros and Cons for each of these publication methods.

Major Publishing Companies
First, you must remember that many New York (and other) major publishing companies have been around for decades, several of them since before the beginning of the modern era of publishing as we know it.

Pros
As a result of their histories major publishers control the industry from acquisition, to editing, to publishing manuscripts, to distribution and sales of books in print.

They have extensive industry connections and resources. In the past they were 'the industry'. It's been their decision as to who and what would be published, promoted, marketed and sold. Until the most recent years of technological advancements in digital printing, these companies literally dictated the ebb and flow of the entire business of print publishing.

These companies have long been able to restrict access to, and distribution within the industry. As a result of the control and money they command, these publishers are not about to relinquish their power position. Major publishers still have the resources and 'clout' to market your book at highly successful levels and onto "best seller" lists.

One of the great attributes of major publishers is their editorial departments. Additionally they have histories, contacts and established relationships vertically and horizontally in business, finance and commerce.

Cons

Large publishers have millions of dollars invested and demand the best possible returns (as they should). That said, they are corporations and as such have the trappings, politics, advantages and disadvantages of corporate America.

As with other industries, people in publishing do business with their friends. It's more often 'who you know' than 'what you've written.' Major publishers are rarely interested in unknown or first time authors. Most novice or first time authors have little or no chance of being noticed without a reputable or credible industry contact. Even then, having an inside contact may not be enough.

As an author, anytime you are involved in professional contract negotiations it's in your best interest to have the advice of attorneys, accountants and/or literary agents. It's been said, "Hire these professionals in direct proportion to the size of the contract you may be signing."

When dealing with publishing corporations, knowledgeable and legal assistance is essential. It's often difficult for authors to separate the business of publishing from the emotions they have invested in their book. When negotiating at these levels you CANNOT do it effectively alone.

Retail bookstore shelf space is at a premium and must generate revenue for book sellers and publishers, period. Publishers count on 'winners' and authors are only as good as their latest selling success. Do you have follow up books? Publishers make money on repeats and referrals (especially word of mouth). They have little interest in "One Hit Wonders."

Even if you are among the elite authorship circles you will do all or much of the promotion legwork at every stage, with every book. This is a business. No one really cares if you are successful or not. (Success being your definition, not theirs.)

Caveat

Many of the major companies in publishing have taken a number of "hits" in the recent recession economy. This has and continues to precipitate changes in personnel and business models.

After intentionally fostering perceptions regarding works by self published authors as inferior in content, presentation and story telling technique, it is only recently and with some reluctance, a few large publishing companies are beginning to look more earnestly at self published authors.

Opinion

Major publishers have resisted the coming digital age and have continued to use antiquated production methods and business models. They are intent on catching up but for many it may be too late or too daunting a task. Technology waits for no-one. Many are beginning to realize that digital printing, "On Demand" printing technologies and distribution channels open to potential world wide markets with direct distribution are here to stay.

Many are also sensing they may not be as indispensible in this new business model with its Internet distribution environment, as they once were or believed. They are no longer the only publication process or "game in town." They will change with the technological times or they will cease to be. Still, they will fight tooth and nail as they resist giving up their established power and control.

These companies have 'called the shots' for a long time and don't intend on giving up control of various aspects of the publishing business or book distribution. As a result of greed and provincial short sightedness, several have "painted themselves into a corner" which is, and will continue to be costly on a number of fronts.

Summary

The rewards of doing business with major publishing companies can be substantial. However, you will relinquish most of the control over your writing. And, in virtually every relationship you will still do the sales and marketing legwork.

The truth is you don't need them anymore. In fact, they may need you in the future more than ever.

Small, Independent, and University Presses

As with their larger counterparts, small, independent and university presses operate similar business platforms and models on a more limited or specialized market scale.

Pros

Due to their size and structure, these companies often specialize in publishing specific genres, areas of interest or works of a particular nature.

Cons

As with their larger competitors, contracts must be analyzed closely. Professional assistance may be in order, and you will still be responsible for your book's promotional legwork and marketing efforts.

Caveat

These publishers may be part of larger entities with mission statements and policies, which restrict their ability to publish outside of a specific area or sphere of influence.

Opinion

When evaluating these publishers, be sure there is a 'connection' between your subject matter and their scope of interest.

Summary

These companies may be easier to work with than their larger commercial brethren and due to their specific audience fulfillment can make for good publishing partners.

Vanity Publishers

So called "Vanity Publishers'" get this label from the concept of "pay for play" or the fact that the author pays the publisher for services rendered.

Pros

Publishers in this category generally offer a 'menu of services' each with an escalating scale of incremental price points associated with its list of tasks, which the publisher will complete for the author.

With vanity publishers the author chooses a 'program' or list of services desired, submits a manuscript according to predetermined formatting and uploading parameters and requirements, and pays the required fees for each set of services. That's it. In return the author receives a final and finished product (the book).

Today, some independent vanity publishers have contact with larger publishers and/or literary agents. There appears to be an increase in cooperation between many of these individuals and groups.

Cons

The primary difference between the major and minor players, versus the vanity publishers is which way the money goes. Major publishers pay the author (usually through an advance) and then with royalties on sales, whereas with a vanity press the author pays for the services selected, which the company provides.

Other contrasts include the size and depth of editorial and marketing departments, as well as the number of associated industry contacts.

In most cases, aside from placement on their websites, any and all marketing activities, promotions or advertising is the individual author's responsibility.

Caveat

Read contracts very closely, especially as they pertain to termination clauses, return of original manuscript materials and post termination sales time frames. Know what the publisher will and will not be responsible for. Contracts will contain rights and obligations for both parties. Knows yours!

Opinion

If you are planning one book, or a limited number of books, but want more potential exposure than selling from your garage or the trunk of your car, contracting with a vanity publisher may be the way to go. You pay for convenience, services and a completed production process. Of the five pathways being discussed here, this is the easiest, because you write the book and submit the manuscript. The vanity publisher will do the rest.

Summary

In choosing a vanity publisher, be cognizant of their strengths and histories. Contact other authors on writing site forums who have used their services, and ask questions. You'll hear opposing sides of the story, but if you dig deep enough you'll discover and know if they might be a match for you and your book.

Self Publishing (often [inaccurately] labeled as "POD")

Before we look at the Pros and Cons of self publishing let's address the issue of "Print On Demand" or "POD". Print On Demand is a digital printing process being used extensively today in the publishing and printing industries. This technology allows a manuscript to be uploaded electronically and then printed digitally at speeds of up to seven hundred pages per minute.

From a cost standpoint, many traditional publishers who have historically used web presses and binding machines in their book production have yet to transition to newer digital technologies. As a result of inroads made into the marketplace by authors using On Demand printers and vanity publishers with access to this technology, larger companies and literary agents initiated a subtle campaign to denigrate independent authors and their works by attaching the label "POD" as if this indicated an inferior product from an unknown author. These tactics and behaviors serve only to reveal the insecurities and fears of those who employ them.

The fact is, POD or Print On Demand is a digital printing method or operation, and nothing more. It denotes no connotation in regard to writers or the quality of their works.

As the title of this book indicates, self publishing is a pathway to publication. You as the writer take full responsibility for everything having to do with your ideas or story going from manuscript to becoming a finished and marketable book, except the actual printing.

The steps required in the self publishing process are not difficult, but they are time consuming, exacting, and can be expensive. You will make mistakes and some can be costly. The most critical components of self publishing are finding the right printer and distribution system for your book(s).

Pros

You have total and complete control over every step of the process and every decision from start to finish, except the actual printing.

Cons

You have total and complete control over every step of the process and every decision from start to finish, except the actual printing. Each step and task you must do, or pay someone else to complete.

Caveat

As a self publisher you will be alone on this journey and every decision you make will ultimately affect your success or failure (in your eyes). You need to have a basic business sense and be willing to actively market your book. Finally, you must have an idea of what you want your writing to accomplish, for your readers and for you.

Opinion

Having attempted for years to query publishers and agents (to no avail) and having contracted my first book with a vanity publisher (to disappointment and misrepresentation) I have since successfully self published twelve trade paperback books and nineteen eBooks. Knowing the steps and process I would now be reluctant to do it any other way. The self publisher gives up nothing, makes all the decisions, takes all the blame and pockets all the profits generated by their work.

Summary

If there is an entrepreneurial spirit in publishing, this is where it lives. The reality is, as a self publisher you are going to end up with approximately twenty five percent of your suggested retail book price and perhaps sixty per cent of your eBook sales price. Out of these figures your costs must be covered.

To self publish successfully, one must be a self starter and motivated to stick with it. The learning curve is steep and you will need to hone multiple skills and/or have resources you can count on to aide in your efforts.

If there is one determiner as to whether or not one should or should not self publish I would say it is this; How many books do you plan to write, publish and attempt to sell? There are amortization stages and points of diminishing return lessons to be learned in self publishing, which are absent in the other pathways being described herein. What you'll want to know is, do your efforts 'pencil out'?

Copy and Bind

Our last pathway is Copy and Bind. Here, you write and finish the manuscript as you wish it to read, then you print copies and have it bound by a business which offers printing and/or binding services. All you have invested is your time, paper, ink, printing and binding costs, and your book is ready to sell. Although Copy and Bind allows you to side step the complexities of the other processes we are discussing, you will still be responsible for all marketing efforts and any taxes generated by the sales of your Copy and Bind book.

Pros

This fifth option of our publication pathways is the easiest, fastest and least expensive way to produce a finished book. If you are a writer you probably already own a typewriter or computer with a word processing program.

You need not worry about Library of Congress Control Numbers, Bar Codes, Copyright Registration, ISBN Number

Assignments, Printer Contracts or Distribution Database Systems.

Cons

The potential market for your book may be limited in scope, geography and distribution. Likewise, you could encounter potential issues, which may arise without legal protection.

Caveat

Copy and Bind is a great way to publish a book for a limited or particular audience. Perhaps you want to publish a cook book with recipes for family members, a church or civic group. This is a viable way to produce an attractive and informative book for readers of provincial interests, with a small investment.

Opinion

There is a likelihood your efforts from the Copy and Bind process may be taken as less than serious by both the publishing industry and the marketplace.

Summary

If you want to write and produce a book as a lasting memory for a specific group of people, Copy and Bind could be just what you're looking for.

Which pathway is best for you? Only you can answer that question. All five pathways require your time, energy and money. You will be doing most if not all of the writing, editing, rewrites, marketing, sales and promotions. Also, any responsibilities related to the business and legal requirements associated with each pathway are ultimately yours to decide and act upon.

It is here you may want to re-evaluate your goals and aspirations as well as your time availability and lifestyle or family obligations. Additionally, you may need to address your current income requirements, job or career restrictions and your ability to take on and complete the myriad of tasks, which are part of the writer's life.

Don't be discouraged. Every writer started out at the same place; with an idea or a story to tell. Many have accomplished their writing dreams. You can too!

Remember, you now have access to a world wide market and there is a segment of buyers out there for every product or service.

CHAPTER 2
The Details

"I have found over my career
there are two absolutes in writing:
Poor writing is still poor writing,
An editor is a necessity."

No matter which of the pathways being described here you may choose to publish your work, it is important to address two authorship factors. Those being; Poor Writing, and the Importance of an Editor.

In every profession there exists a modicum of decorum. For writers this relates to content presentation. Your responsibility, both to your readers and to the language is that your writing consists minimally of accepted and correct usage.

While your story and its context may require 'poetic license' to give it a unique and solely "you" authorship, a fundamental and familiar understanding of generally accepted rules pertaining to the language; mechanics, tense, punctuation, spelling, parts of speech, idioms, axioms, et al. is necessary. If your desire is to publish and be taken seriously as a writer your work should adhere to proper language usage.

"Twitter" and mobile device style "texting" may be decipherable by its denizens, but in most cases is inappropriate for book publishing. Bastardization of the language may be acceptable among group sycophants and cronies, but it is unacceptable to educated readers and most publishers.

Written language should flow, inspire, create and entice. It should not disrupt the reader or fail to express correctly the author's thoughts and words. As William Shawn, long time editor at *The New Yorker* magazine and editor of many well known twentieth century authors commented, "Amid chaos of images, we value coherence. We believe in the printed word. And we believe in clarity. And we believe in immaculate syntax. And in the beauty of the English language."

In my role as a reviewer of other authors' works, nothing is more disconcerting than to have the flow of the story interrupted by a stumbling through or over, poorly presented and inappropriate language usage.

Simply said, poor writing is still poor writing. The task of being an effective communicator and writer is difficult enough, without hampering your efforts through misuse of the language. Don't begin your writing with 'strikes against you.' Do yourself and your readers a favor, write within the bounds of correct language usage. Your publisher and your readers will thank you.

Now what's all this about an editor?
At prominent publishing companies and those with histories of success, one of the most valuable assets they possess is an editorial department.

In book publishing's heyday of the twentieth century, many of the literary world's most respected authors were in need of the editor's hand. In some instances it was actually the editor who made the story's manuscript cohesive and readable. Putting corrected and finishing touches on works and stories often helped make a book a best seller and its author highly sought after.

As writers we are sometimes so close to our work as it is read and re-read, that we read right through our errors. At every level of writing, an editor is a necessity. Be open to corrections and advice, for once your book is printed, every error and mistake requiring change is costly in both time and money; spent and lost. An editor may not make you a better author, but he or she can help you become a better writer. A well edited book may not prove helpful in sales, but it can't hurt, as will a poorly edited or unedited book.

Although technologies and the Internet have opened the world to would be writers, the sheer numbers of books being produced and entering the marketplace on a daily basis makes for fierce competition.

As with our statements pertaining to poor writing versus well written material, correct language use honed by good editing can make the difference with a prospective reader in their decision to buy.

In the business of writing, as with other consumer focused businesses, a pleased and satisfied reader may tell one or more friends about your book, but a reader who has struggled with the story because of uncorrected editorial mistakes, may tell everyone. Don't shoot yourself in the foot prior to ever pulling your book from its holster. Keep in mind the importance of good, better and best writing under the tutelage and assistance of professional editing.

If you write for publication, your name will be on your works and the world will know. Here the old adage is as applicable as ever: "You never get a second chance to make a first impression." This is true of your writing as well.

CHAPTER 3
Subjectivity and Rejection

"It is advantageous to an author
that his book should be attacked
as well as praised. Fame is a shuttlecock.
If it be struck only at one end of the room,
it will soon fall to the ground. To keep it up,
it must be struck at both ends."
~Samuel Johnson

If you have taken that leap of faith, deciding to publish and place your book on the open market for public critique and consumption, be forewarned, you are about to face two seemingly insurmountable obstacles to your success as a published author.

The first is Subjectivity. This is a double edged sword. There are just as many likes and dislikes among readers, as there are readers. Not everyone who is exposed to your work will be impressed or accepting. The key is to discover who your readers and fans are, where they are located and how you can become accessible to them.

The second is Rejection. It is this single word with its deep rooted emotional context for each of us, which can and does wreak havoc upon the psyche of many, particularly those in the arts.

Authors pour themselves, their beliefs, attitudes and perceptions into their work. They then risk being rejected by ones, twos, threes and thousands as they lay bare publicly their thoughts, ideas and opinions in the stories and books they've written.

It is the dreaded anticipation of, or actual hearing the word "No" in response to their works, which often paralyzes writers and keeps them in the shadows away from the pathways to publishing.

These two, Subjectivity and Rejection, are inescapable and present for every writer, at each stage of their career and with every book they author. So, you may ask, are there any remedies for these two henchmen? The answer is yes. Your relief may be found in Tenacity and Belief.

This is your life. Writing is your choice. Remember, everyone has an opinion and many are ready to broadcast theirs. So be it. You are writing for those with whom you have a connection and common interest. These are the people who will follow your work; becoming fans, supporters, readers and buyers.

This type of effort requires tenacity. As a writer you consistently invest time regularly attending to your manuscripts; writing, editing, rewriting, proofing, researching, studying, etc.

Writing is a process with many aspects, all which need constant attention along the path to becoming a finished book. Writing takes perseverance. Successful writing also requires belief on your part with regard to your work, your efforts and the plethora of different tasks you as a self published author must accomplish.

For most, seeing is believing. For some, believing is seeing. Act on your beliefs and focus, to finish your book waiting in the wings.

CHAPTER 4
Two Hats

"Like it or not, every successful writer
must wear two hats;
Author and Salesperson."

Have you ever heard anyone say, "I'm not a salesperson." Trust them, they're telling you the truth. Surveys show that 'death' ranks number two, behind the fear of public speaking. This does not bode well for writers who concur, "I am not a salesperson."

We live in a time where image is king and there's a market for every product or service. (I've owned more than one 'Hula Hoop' but never a 'Pet Rock' or 'Mood Ring'.) As with our previous discussion involving the fortitude needed to willingly expose your work in the forefront of the public eye, you must also be prepared to actively sell and market your book. In our Mega-Market world, sales are the lifeblood that keeps economies running. As an author, no sales effort on behalf of your book is going to be more important than your own. And sell you must.

Of all the tasks ahead you will take responsibility for as a self published author, one of the most critical is that of marketer. In this role you will need to identify your target group of readers and proceed to get your book in front of them in every way possible and as often as you can.

If you feel unsure or inept at releasing your works to the public, *or* you cannot bring yourself to market and sell your book, you might consider the hobby stage or the easier Copy and Bind method we talked of earlier. Here again there's no guilt in recognizing your strengths and weaknesses, and playing to your strengths. That's smart business, even for writers.

Remember this, sales is a skill set which can be learned. Salespeople are not born, they are taught. Sales success is practiced behavior. With a little help and guidance you can become more effective at selling and marketing your book.

Perhaps the most convenient way to share and start selling your book is to make use of Internet blogging venues and writing web sites where you can post excerpts from and information about your works and content. In this way you will be in front of potential readers and buyers without direct interaction, and at the same time your postings may advance your entrée and positioning onto search engines such as Google and Yahoo.

Today, the importance of a professional looking and informative, easy to navigate web site with a shopping cart cannot be overstated. Current studies show that seventy percent of

Internet users say the World Wide Web is their first choice when deciding on the purchase of products and services. Not only do you want and need exposure, it's essential that you have a 'home' where people can find your book, learn about you the author, and purchase. The necessity of having an author web site would apply to all of our publishing pathways, no matter which one you might employ.

Don't forget about social media and writing sites. These can give you world wide exposure for limited or no cost. Your ultimate goal as a marketer is to garner the maximum amount of presence with your target reading audience, at the lowest dollar investment or no cost to you.

Marketing monies are not recoupable and therefore can be an expense with no end in sight. Have a realistic marketing campaign and budget in place. If you invest in a program which doesn't pay for itself or generate sales and income, examine it closely before continuing it. There are different marketing opportunities and avenues you can try. Put those which don't serve you effectively on the back burner or discontinue and find alternatives.

As stated before you as the author will be doing most, if not all the marketing on your own behalf. It is crucial that any costs associated with these efforts be free, or as inexpensive as possible.

Even if you are nervous or intimidated, remember, you are the expert concerning your story. Take your passion for the story you've written and transfer that energy to talking points surrounding the connections between your book and your reading audience.

Now here's more good news! There are more market segments, specialized areas of interest and buyers than ever before, and you have more access to them than ever before! They're out there waiting for you and your book.

CHAPTER 5
Who Are You?

"There's nothing to writing.
All you do is sit down at a typewriter
and open a vein."
~Red Smith

Here are a set of reflective questions one should ask and answer honestly about their role as a writer.

What is my publishing goal?

As a writer - my job is to . . . . . what?

Who am I? (As a writer)

To me writing success looks like . . . what?

What market segment is mine?
How can I explore it and exploit it for its value?
Who is my audience?

Can and will I fulfill anticipations and expectations by staying relevant to my reading audience?

Am I a "One Hit Wonder"?

What is my purpose and intent in writing?

What is it I want to accomplish?
Make a living? Leave a legacy?

The circular reference in writing is; Write, Edit, Re-Write. Market. Write, Edit, Re-Write. Market. Make this your mantra and your practice.

Now that you have an idea of your role as a writer, when do you start making money from your energies?

Well, know this -
The only difference between your book and a best seller is the number of zero's after that first one sold.
So, how do we get those zeros?

Here are ten questions which can help you both answer and determine how many zero's you may add after that first "one".

1. Am I a story teller?
People love a good story (one they identify with). Does mine give hope, guidance, escape, release . . . what?

2. Is what I write memorable?
Does my work strike a chord or touch a nerve with readers?

3. Will readers want more?

4. Will readers be endeared and excited enough to seek out my work? And tell others about it?

5. Am I ready, willing and able to withstand public criticism?

6. How far and how often am I willing to travel to be in front of my readers?

7. Am I willing to participate in reading and writing groups?

8. What makes my work different or unique?

9. What is my hook? What is my platform?

10. Can and will readers be able to identify with my work?

CHAPTER 6
Dollars and Sense
(Not a One Time Investment)

"Almost anyone can be an author;
the business is to collect money and fame
from this state of being."
~A.A. Milne

We are preparing to start our step by step process to self publishing, but before we do we should look at one more piece of information: Costs. Investment dollars. Do they make sense?

As mentioned before, there are costs associated with publication of your book and these can run from a fistful to thousands. Remember, the more involved your publishing and marketing efforts, the more income or reserves you will need to be able to draw upon and invest.

The Basics. These would include a typewriter or computer with a word processing program, paper, ink, dictionary, stamps, envelopes and digital camera. (If your book includes pictures, graphs, tables, illustrations or other visuals not accessible elsewhere for free or purchase). The other variable to keep in mind is that you will need to achieve all tasks, either on your own or with assistance, be they paid or unpaid.

The following associated costs must be considered in order to have a finished book ready to sell.

Copy and Bind Pathway;
Writing; Editing, Proofreading
Formatting, Cover Designs
Web Site; Design, Hosting, Updates
Shopping Cart Service
Bank Account

Self Publishing Pathway;
Editor, Proof Reader relationship
Graphic Artist relationship
Formatting relationship
Web site relationships
Printer relationship
Distributor relationship
Marketing assistance
Travel expenses
Fees (contests, reviews, competitions)
Local, state and federal business licenses,
fees and taxes
Corporation, LLC or Sole Proprietor costs for
legal and maintenance fees, filings
Returned book costs

Major Publishers, Small, Independent, University Presses or Vanity Pathways;
While contracts with these businesses will cover the production of your finished book, I would suggest a list comparable to that shown above for a functioning web site, travel,

marketing, promotion and advertising expenses, for your direct sales and inquiries.

The amount of money you may need to invest on your own behalf when working with these publishers will vary with their size, business dictates, services and commitments. Be sure you are apprised of all expenses and costs you may be liable for, prior to signing contracts. Remember, even with contracts in effect, you will be doing most if not all of the marketing, promoting and selling of your book.

Additionally, regardless of which pathway you choose, you will have recurring costs with each book you publish. Here are scenarios relating to real world publishing costs for many authors:

Major Publisher;
Publisher pays the author an advance against earnings, and royalties on books sold (less returns). Author pays commissions and fees to agents, lawyers, accountants and is responsible for personal expenses.

Small, Independent, University Presses;
Each contract may vary in arrangements. Usually no, or small advance, royalties on sales (less returns). Author pays personal expenses, representation costs.

Vanity Publishers;

"Program" choices range from $0 to $3000, (you pay). This wide spread is dependent upon the services the author contracts for with an individual company. For example, a $500 program <u>might</u> include; cover design, ISBN acquisition and printing, plus fifteen copies of your finished book. Again, each publisher offers different 'menus' of services with differing cost structures. Compare and contrast what you get for your investment, according to your particular needs.

Self Publishing;

A minimum investment if the author only needed the bare essentials might be in the range of $350 + per book. At a minimum you'll need; cover formatting, title set up, one proof copy, PCN and ISBN acquisitions, copyright registration, ten finished copies and annual fees per book for ISBN listing, web site domain renewal and distributor data base listing.

A more realistic figure would be $750 - 1000+ depending upon the amount and extent of prepublication professional assistance needed (see these additional costs listed in chapter 7.)

Copy and Bind;

Usually less than $25 presuming you don't need to purchase hardware, software or ink cartridges. With those items in place all you need is paper, paper cutter and binding (spiral) service with laminated front and back covers.

In addition to that which is shown, an author must factor in advertising and marketing expenses on the back end.

CHAPTER 7
Step by Step to Self Publishing Success

"And Away, We Go"
~Jackie Gleason

So, after all this preparation, are you ready? I've published twelve books this way. YOU CAN TOO!

In this chapter you'll learn the process and steps needed to self publish your book. This step-by-step guide is presuming you wish to "Self Publish" not Copy and Bind. Although Copy and Bind is a method of self publishing, it is unrelated to "Self Publishing" as we are discussing here.

First write, edit, rewrite, *ad nausea*. Take the final draft of your manuscript and make a hard copy backup. Upload and save all manuscript word documents. Make a cyberspace copy and a disk copy. (I find it's best to have a folder with all related work for each project from start to finish in its own place, with all changes and backup.)

Have a plan, a direction, a goal and a budget. If you need their assistance, find an editor, a graphic artist, a content formatter and web site designer. Find a printer. Determine a distribution system.

Here are additional questions you will want to address and have answered prior to contracting with a printer.

Will your book be hard cover or paperback? Will it be black and white, or include color printing? What size page do you desire? Your page count will determine your spine size. What choices does your printer offer? These all need to be asked of the printer you choose.

Your digital On Demand printer will have the capability to produce your book in a number of different sizes and bindings (hard cover, paperback, etc.) For each there are different set up requirements and cost price points. Check with your printer.

Have the editor reading, the artist working on your cover concept and visuals. Have your web site under construction. Compare printers and distributor services. Contract for services.

If you are unable to obtain assistance in your immediate geographic area to fulfill the above stated professional needs, go to writing web sites and forums on the Internet for your genre. There you will usually find these services offered and available for hire, or hyperlinks to these services.

Before you can submit your manuscript disk or upload your manuscript electronically, your chosen printer will advise you as to the required formatting, embeds, fonts, visuals, cover requirements, sizing, etc. needed for printing.

With all tasks complete, turn your manuscript and cover designs over to your formatter and graphics designer for final preparations required to upload.

If a publisher (you) sells their books on their own and are not trying to place them in stores, libraries or with wholesalers, No ISBN is required. However, if you intend to distribute through retailers online, brick and mortar or wholesale, an ISBN is essential.

An ISBN, or International Standard Book Number is a unique numeric commercial book identifier based upon the 9-digit Standard Book Numbering (SBN) code and refers to the identification number for a particular book. If you need ISBNs, contact R. R. Bowker, U.S. ISBN Agency to purchase the ISBN required for your book(s). Bowker will notify you when the ISBN for your book has been assigned. There are other ISBN "brokers" however, we have used Bowker for ten years and they have always been prompt and responsive.

Next, contact the Library of Congress in Washington, D.C. or at their website on-line and fill out the forms necessary to request a PCN (Pre-assigned Control Number). There is no charge, but you will need to register and provide the requested information.

As mentioned, there are several ISBN vendors. Likewise, there are numerous printers and distributors you may choose to do business with. We use Lightning Source, Inc. for our printing and Ingram Content Group for our distribution. Both are located in La Vergne, TN. (See appendix contacts list).

When you have both your ISBN and PCN, go to the title page of your manuscript and add these. (See the title page of this book for example). If your intent is to market through wholesale and retail channels, be sure your book's back cover displays the ISBN bar code identifier. Your graphic designer should add this identifier for you during the design process. This bar code identifier is necessary for sales and inventory control at all major retailers such as Amazon, Barnes and Noble, Wal Mart, Target, et al.

You may or may not wish to add the suggested retail price on your book. Your printer will provide you with the information on making this addition to your ISBN bar code on your book's back cover. We do not print price bar codes on our books. This allows retailers to sell our books at competitive and comparable prices for our genres, within their particular markets and for their particular customers. Our wholesale prices are standard, our retail pricing may vary.

Now that your manuscript and covers are finished and formatted, go back and proofread it one more time. Have another person read it also. When you are positive it is in its final form, it's ready for submission.

Take Notice! Whatever you submit to your printer as your manuscript is exactly the content as it will be printed; typos, errors and mistakes included. For this reason, we order a 'Proof Copy' for a final inspection before we go to multiple copy print.

If you have requested a 'Proof Copy', it will be sent to you as the finished book. Take time to peruse it carefully. Reread it. Have your editor and another person read it as well. Look for mistakes, cover to cover. When you are satisfied, submit your final approval for printing.

 You will need to order at least five finished copies;
Two for the Library of Congress Catalogue Dept.
Two for the Library of Congress Copyright Office.
One for yourself.

Now obviously there are other people; family, friends, book stores, business and group or association acquaintances to whom you may wish to give complimentary or review copies. We find that our first order is generally fifty books. We immediately use twenty five to thirty for these types of obligations.

<u>Self Publishing Costs</u>
(Approximate, your investments will vary)
<u>Essential Hardware</u> (costs vary)
Typewriter and/or Computer with word processing program
Printer
Paper
Printer cartridge(s)
Dictionary
Stamps
Envelopes
Folders

<u>Web site(s)</u>
Web site design and development
Web site maintenance and changes
Web site domain registrations and renewals
Shopping Cart (costs vary)

<u>Additional Costs, Printed Books</u>
(Prices shown are actual or approximations)
Editor (varies)
Cover(s), Art, Graphics (varies)
Content Formatting (varies)
Printer Contract (varies)
Distributor Contract (varies)
ISBN $125.00 and up
Title Set Up $75.00 (varies by printer)
Content, Text or Graphics Changes $45.00

each revision (varies by printer)
Proof Copies $30.00 ea. (varies by printer)
Copyright Registration $35.00 and up
Initial order of fifty books $200.00 (varies by book size and type)
Distribution Database listing $12.00/book./yr.
Bowker $25.00 (annual renewal listing/book)
Complimentary Copies (Preview/Review)
Advertising (varies by medium, frequency)
Wholesale Discounts (generally 30-55%)
Attorney, CPA, travel, exhibits/fairs (costs vary)

As you can see, your investment is substantial and can escalate dramatically depending on the degree of professional assistance you require. Generally speaking, a book start to finish will cost in the minimum range of $350.00 and up.

Self Publishing is neither easy nor inexpensive. You are looking at months, perhaps years of work, research and writing, at a cost of hundreds, if not thousands of investment dollars.

EBook conversions are as easy as uploading a file, but heed the formatting requirements and follow the instructions of the converter to insure your book will flow properly for reading ease on each particular e-reader devise (i.e. Adobe, Kindle, iPad).

Today it's possible to upload and sell your book in eBook formats and forego the entire printing process. You will still need an

ISBN identifier, a distributor, proper cover and text formatting for upload, Library of Congress control number and copyright registration (if you desire Library of Congress cataloguing and copyright protection).

You will also need to plan for advertising and marketing. Even in this 'eBook only' case I would still suggest an editor and/or proofreader be used.

There are a variety of e-reader devices on the market and you'll want the maximum your exposure and purchasing availability for use on as many devises as possible. For eBook distribution I would suggest exploring relationships with the following, or other similar companies.
Ingram Digital, Google Book Partners, Amazon, Barnes and Noble, Diesel eBook Store and Smashwords. With these eBook partners your book can be converted to every (current)
e-reader device.

Before the first chapter of this book I made a comment about the future growth potential of eBooks as a vehicle of electronically disseminated information. If you intend to self publish in eBook formats know that there exists a "Sword of Damocles" you must contend with if you use Amazon as a distributor. The price you set for your eBooks will also adjust your printed book (paperback and hard cover) prices as well. You will need to use Amazon's price and royalty structures for eBook publications as the baseline determinate for your printed book pricing. To learn more about this topic, go to Amazon online and read its Kindle publishing guidelines as it pertains to royalties.

After all the work, time, effort and energy to produce a viable and attractive edition of your book, what is your reward?
Your thoughts, ideas, opinions, stories and words will be published for the world to read. Your book will also have its literary place henceforth in annals of the future. Additionally, you will be leaving a legacy or make a living, perhaps both.

On the following page is a scheduled checklist for your use to insure this step-by-step process goes smoothly and all steps are accomplished.

<u>Step-by-Step Self Publishing Checklist</u>

- ✍ Complete Manuscript
- ✍ Proofread Thoroughly
- ✍ Have Others Proofread
- ✍ Make needed changes
- ✍ Contract with Printer
- ✍ Contract with Distributor
- ✍ Contract with Editor, have manuscript edited
- ✍ Contract with Artist(s)/Graphics: covers, et al., have graphics completed
- ✍ Contract with web site designer, have web site constructed, up and running
- ✍ Contract with Submission Formatter
- ✍ Order ISBN
- ✍ Order PCN
- ✍ Add ISBN/ PCN to title page
- ✍ Have final manuscript formatted according to printer requirements
- ✍ Have final cover and visuals formatted according to printer requirements
- ✍ Submit finished Text, Content, Covers
- ✍ Receive Proof Copy
- ✍ Submit changes (if any)
- ✍ Approve final Proof Copy
- ✍ Order books / Receive books
- ✍ Promote / Sell books
- ✍ Send two copies to the Library of Congress Catalogue Dept. within 30 days
- ✍ Send two copies to Library of Congress Copyright Office within 45 days
- ✍ Contract with eBook distributors
- ✍ Upload content and covers in eBook formats to eBook distributors
- ✍ Implement Marketing, Advertising

Appendix
Self Published Books
Self Published Authors
Rejections

Contacts:
Bowker, LLC.
Library of Congress
Lightning Source Inc.
Ingram Content Group, Inc.
Ingram Digital
Google Book Partners
Diesel eBooks
Amazon
Barnes and Noble
Smashwords

Famous Self Published Books
Joy of Cooking by Irma S. Rombauer

When I Am an Old Woman I Shall Wear Purple by Sandra Haldeman-Martz

Life's Little Instruction Book by H. Jackson Brown, Jr.

Robert's Rules of Order by Henry M. Robert

The Bridges of Madison County by Robert James Waller

What Color is Your Parachute by Richard Bolles

Remembrance of Things Past by Marcel Proust

Ulysses by James Joyce

Adventures of Peter Rabbit by Beatrix Potter

A Time to Kill by John Grisham

The Wealthy Barber by David Chilton

In Search of Excellence by Tom Peters

The Celestine Prophecy by James Redfield

The Elements of Style by William Strunk, Jr.

<u>Famous Self Published Authors</u>
Deepak Chopra
Gertrude Stein
Zane Grey
Upton Sinclair
Carl Sandburg
Ezra Pound
Mark Twain
Edgar Rice Burroughs
Stephen Crane
Bernard Shaw
Anais Nin
Thomas Paine
Virginia Wolff
e.e. Cummings
Edgar Allen Poe
Rudyard Kipling
Henry David Thoreau
Benjamin Franklin
Walt Whitman
Alexandre Dumas
William E.B. DuBois

Rejected by Publishers
Pearl S. Buck; *The Good Earth* 14 times

Norman Mailer; *The Naked and the Dead*
12 times

Patrick Dennis; *Auntie Mame* 15 times

George Orwell; *Animal Farm*

Richard Bach; *Jonathan Livingston Seagull*
20 times

Joseph Heller; *Catch-22* (22 times !)

Mary Higgins Clark; first short story 40 times

Alex Haley, (before Roots) 200 rejections

Robert Persig; *Zen and the Art of Motorcycle Maintenance* 121 times

John Grisham; *A Time to Kill* 15 publishers and 30 agents (he ended up publishing it himself).

Chicken Soup for the Soul, 33 times

Dr. Seuss, 24 times

Louis L'Amour, 200 rejections

Jack London, 600 before his first story

John Creasy, 774 rejections before selling his first story. He went on to write 564 books, using fourteen names.

Jerzy Kosinski, 13 agents and 14 publishers rejected his best-selling novel when he submitted it under a different name, including Random House (the original publisher).

During his entire lifetime, Herman Melville's timeless classic, *Moby Dick* sold only 3,715 copies.

Stephen King's first four novels were rejected. "This guy from Maine sent in this novel over the transom" said Bill Thompson his former Editor at Doubleday. Mr. Thompson, sensing something there, asked to see subsequent novels, but still rejected the next three. However, King withstood the rejection, and Mr. Thompson finally bought the fifth novel, despite his colleague's lack of enthusiasm, for $2,500. It was called *Carrie*.

Contact Information:

R.R. Bowker, LLC. ISBN Agent
http://www.isbn.org/standards/home/isbn/us/ind
ex.asp

Bowkerlink (for publishers with accounts)
http://bowkerlink.com/corrections/common/hom
e.asp

Library of Congress
http://www.loc.gov/index.html

Library of Library of Congress
(Publishers Page [PCN Assignment Numbers])
http://www.loc.gov/publish/

Library of Congress Catalogue Dept.
http://pcn.loc.gov/

Library of Congress Copyright Registration
http://www.copyright.gov/

Printer:
Lighting Source, Inc. US
1246 Heil Quaker Blvd.
La Vergne, TN USA 37086
http://lightningsource.com/
Email: inquiry@lightningsource.com

Distributor:
Ingram Content Group, Inc.
1 Ingram Blvd.
La Vergne, TN 37086
http://www.ingrambook.com/
Email: Inquiry@ingramcontent.com

eBooks
Ingram Digital
http://www.ingramdigital.com/publishers/

Google Book Partners
http://books.google.com/googlebooks/publishers
.html

Diesel eBook Store
http://www.diesel-ebooks.com/

Smashwords
http://www.smashwords.com/

Amazon
http://www.amazon.com/

Barnes and Noble
http://www.barnesandnoble.com/

Branch Isole is the author of nineteen books. Born in Osaka Japan, Branch traveled extensively growing up calling many places home. Finishing high school in Southern California, he went on to graduate from Texas State University, attended graduate school at the University of Houston and received an M.A. Theology degree from Trinity Bible College and Seminary.

Branch Isole's catalogue of work includes books, eBooks, greeting cards and inspirational gift mats, available at

www.branchisole.com
www.manaopublishing.com

Other books by Branch Isole
Poetic Prose Series

Heartstrings of Illusion ©
Distractions and Deceit in Poetic Prose
ISBN 978-0982658543

Dreams and Schemes ©
Tales and Tattles in Poetic Prose
ISBN 978-0982658550

In The Margins ©
where truth lies
ISBN 978-0982658536

Eclectic Electricity ©
unknown poet's parade
ISBN 978-0982658512

Turn Of A Phrase ©
Pivotal Positions in Poetic Prose
ISBN 978-0982658505

Saccharin and Plastic Band Aids ©
Comments in Poetic Prose
ISBN 978-0974769288

Messages In A Bottle ©
Inspirations in Poetic Prose
ISBN 978-0974769295

Reflections On Chrome ©
Parking Lot Confessions in Poetic Prose
ISBN 978-0974769257

Postcards from the Line of Demarcation ©
Points of Separation in Poetic Prose
ISBN 978-0974769264

Seeds of Mana'o ©
Thoughts, Ideas and Opinions in Poetic Prose
ISBN 978-0974769219

Barking Geckos ©
Stories and Observations in Poetic Prose
ISBN 978-0974769226